Planets in Our Solar System

VENUS

by Jody S. Rake

PEBBLE
a capstone imprint

Pebble Explore is published by Pebble, an imprint of Capstone.
1710 Roe Crest Drive
North Mankato, Minnesota 56003
www.capstonepub.com

Library of Congress Cataloging-in-Publication Data is available on the Library of Congress website.
ISBN: 978-1-9771-2392-3 (hardcover)
ISBN: 978-1-9771-2692-4 (paperback)
ISBN: 978-1-9771-2429-6 (eBook PDF)

Summary: The second brightest object in the sky, after the moon is Venus. It's also the only planet named after a woman. Learn more about bright, beautiful Venus, named for the Roman goddess of love and beauty.

Image Credits
Getty Images: Hulton Archive, 7, Ron Miller/Stocktrek Images, 12, Santi Visalli Inc, 15, The Asahi Shimbun, 22; iStockphoto: shaunl, 28; NASA: JPL, 14, JPL-Caltech/ESA, 18, JSC, 21; Newscom: Aoes Medialab/esa/Hand Out/picture alliance/dpa/picture, 23, ESA/INAF-IASF/UPI, 19; Science Source: Detlev van Ravenswaay, 27, Gary Hincks, 26; Shutterstock: Dotted Yeti, Cover Left, guardiano007, 1, Johan Swanepoel, 6, Macrovector, 10, MattLphotography, 5, NASA images, Cover, Pavel Gabzdyl, Back Cover, Peyker, 17, Steve Allen, 13, Trifonenkolvan, 11, Vadim Sadovski, 9, Zwiebackesser, 8; Wikimedia: NASA, 25, NASA/JPL/David Seal, 16

Design Elements
Shutterstock: Arcady, BLACKDAY, ebes, LynxVector, phipatbig, Stefan Holm, veronchick_84

Editorial Credits
Editor: Alison Deering; Designer: Jennifer Bergstrom; Media Researcher: Tracy Cummins; Production Specialist: Tori Abraham

Printed in the United States of America.
PA117

Table of Contents

Words in **bold** are in the glossary.

Venus, "the Evening Star"

A bright star appears in the sky just after the sun sets. It does not twinkle. It is not a star at all. It is Venus.

Venus is one of the brightest objects in our sky. Only the sun and the moon are brighter. Venus is also called "the evening star."

Venus looks bright white from space. It is covered with clouds. Sunlight bounces off these clouds. Then it bounces back into space. We can see this light bouncing off Venus.

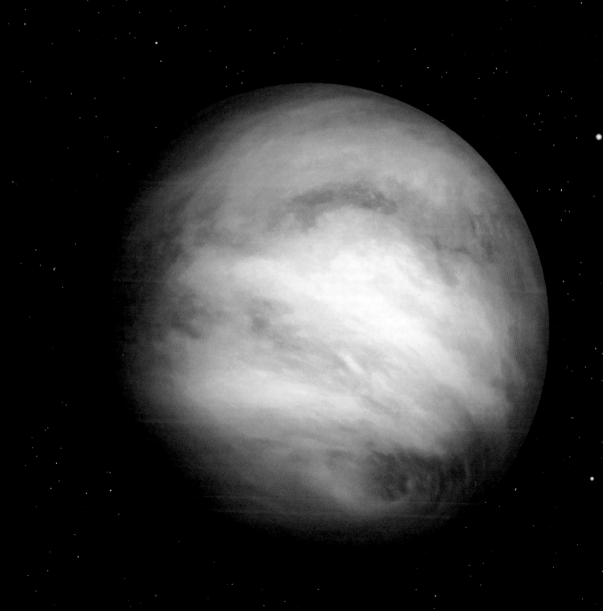

Earth's Neighbor

Venus comes closer to Earth than any other planet. Its path around the sun is closest to Earth's. But it also moves far away. Sometimes Mercury is closer to Earth.

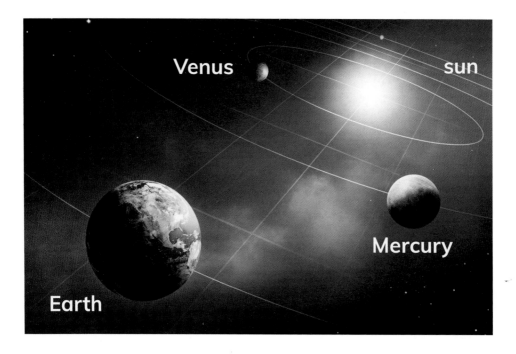

Venus   sun

Mercury

Earth

Galileo and his telescope

We do not know when Venus was first discovered. People have known about it for thousands of years.

A **scientist** was the first person to see Venus. His name was Galileo. He spotted it more than 400 years ago. He used a tool called a **telescope**.

Venus was named after the Roman goddess of love and beauty. It is the only planet named for a woman. Maybe it was named this because it is so bright and beautiful.

The Roman goddess Venus

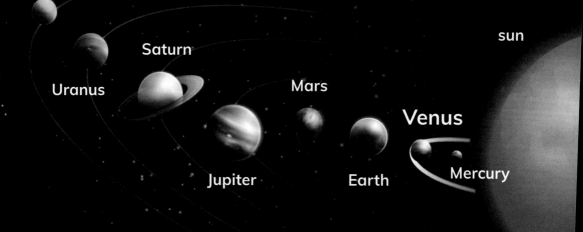

Uranus
Saturn
Mars
sun
Venus
Jupiter
Earth
Mercury

Venus is the second planet from the sun. It moves in a path around the sun. This is called an **orbit**. Venus's path is almost a perfect circle.

Venus moves very quickly. If a plane could fly as fast, it would circle Earth three times in one hour!

Clouds and Beyond

Venus's surface is made of rock. But we can't see it from space. It is hidden by clouds.

Beneath the clouds, Venus is mostly gray. It has a thick, cloudy **atmosphere**. Imagine you were standing on the planet. The sun would make the land look orange.

Maxwell Montes on Venus

Denali, the highest mountain in North America

Venus has many mountains. The tallest is Maxwell Montes. It is almost twice as high as Denali. That is the highest mountain in North America.

Craters on Venus

Venus has about 900 large holes. These holes are called **craters**. They were made when giant space rocks hit the planet.

Venus's holes all have names. Crater Mead is the largest. It is named after an American scientist. Her name was Margaret Mead.

Margaret Mead

Clouds move quickly on Venus.

Venus has no moons. It also has no rings. We can only see its clouds.

Strong winds blow the clouds. They move around the planet all the time. They move very quickly. It takes five Earth days for the clouds to go around the planet once.

The thick clouds hold in the sun's heat. This makes Venus the hottest planet. It is hot enough to melt the metal **lead**.

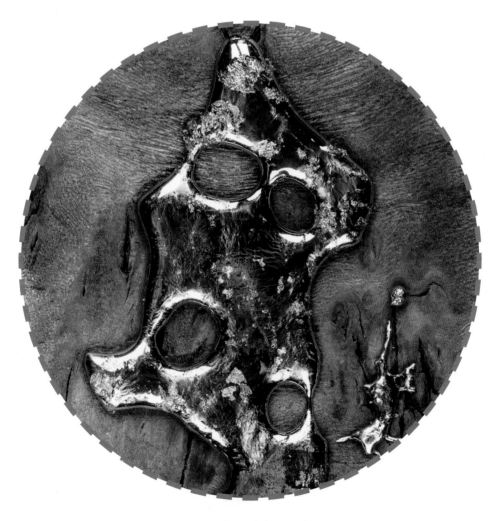

Melted lead

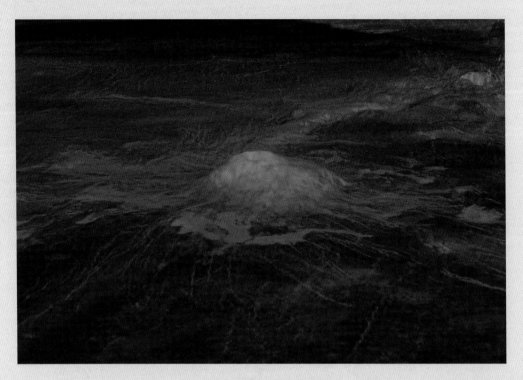

Venus has a very hot surface.

Venus's atmosphere has many layers.
They all have different temperatures.
The surface is the hottest.

Farther up, it gets cooler. In the clouds, the temperature is about the same as on Earth.

Venus's clouds reflect sunlight.

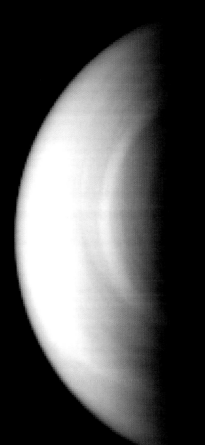

Dark areas show thick clouds.

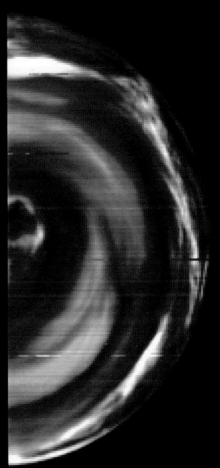

Exploring Venus

No one has ever been to Venus. But many spacecraft have gone to explore it. The first one flew past more than 50 years ago.

In 1982, a spacecraft landed on Venus. It sent back the first color pictures. It lasted about two hours before the planet's heat wrecked it.

Another craft began to circle the planet in 1990. It had special tools to see past the clouds. It sent information back to Earth for four years.

A spacecraft starts its journey to Venus.

In 2005, a new craft took off. It arrived at Venus in 2006. It sent information to Earth for almost eight years. Contact was lost in 2014.

A spacecraft takes off for Venus in 2010.

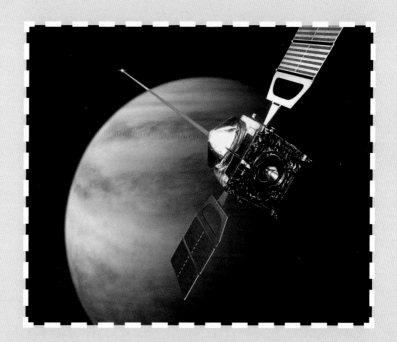

A spacecraft circles Venus.

The newest craft launched in 2010. It circled the sun for five years. In 2015, it started circling Venus.

Like Earth, but Different

Venus is only a little smaller than Earth. Imagine you could **tunnel** straight through both planets. The tunnel through Venus would be only a little shorter than one through Earth.

The two planets have almost the same **gravity**. Let's say you weigh 100 pounds (45 kilograms) on Earth. You would weigh about 90 pounds (41 kg) on Venus.

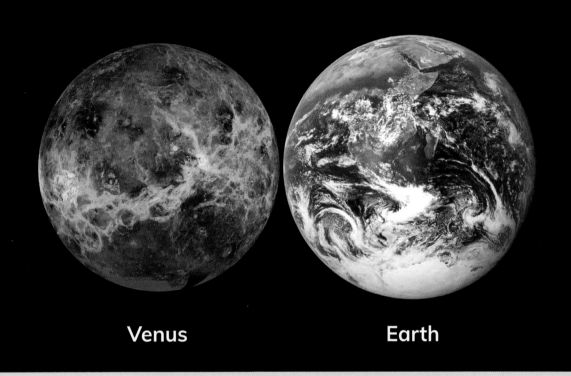

Venus   Earth

People cannot live on Venus.
It is too hot. The planet has no air.
The atmosphere is mainly deadly
gases. It is very heavy! People would
be crushed. It would feel like you were
deep under the ocean.

Venus spins very slowly. That means it has the longest day of any planet. It takes 243 Earth days to make one spin. That is one day on Venus!

Venus also spins backward. The sun rises in the west. It sets in the east.

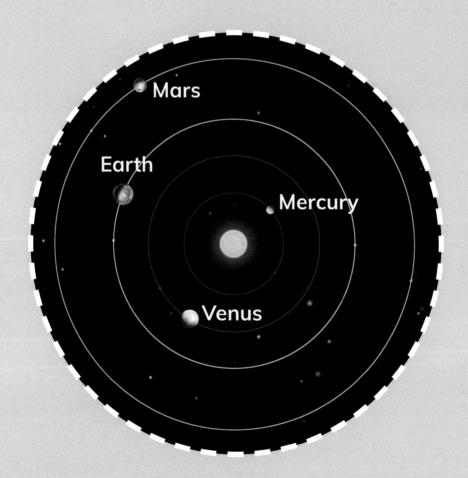

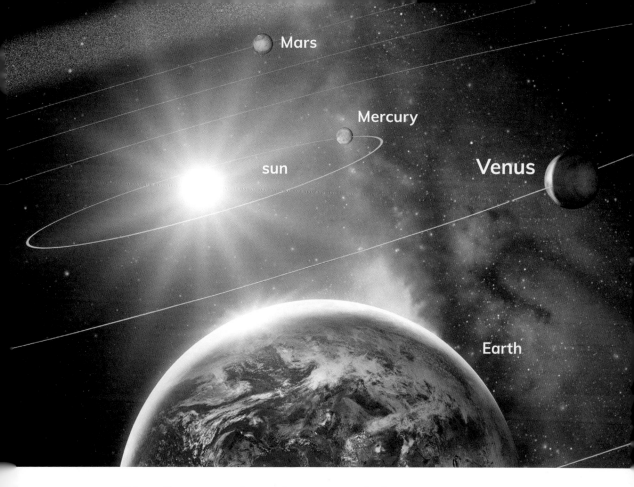

The four rocky planets of the inner solar system circle the sun.

Venus moves around the sun quickly. Earth moves around the sun once in 365 days. That's one year. Venus does this in about 225 days. That means a day on Venus is just a little longer than a year.

When to See Venus

Venus can be seen from Earth most of the year. During some months, you can see it before the sun rises. During other months, you can see it after the sun sets.

For two months each Earth year, Venus is on the opposite side of the sun. Then we can't see it at all.

Venus in the
night sky

Fast Facts

Name:
Venus

Location:
2nd planet from the sun

Planet Type:
rocky

Discovered:
unknown; first seen through telescope in 1610

Moons:

Glossary

atmosphere (AT-muh-sfeer)—layer of gases that surrounds some planets, dwarf planets, and moons

crater (KRAY-tur)—a large hole in the ground caused by crashing rocks

gas (GASS)—something that is not solid or liquid and does not have a definite shape

gravity (GRAV-uh-tee)—a force that pulls objects together

lead (LED)—a soft, gray metal

orbit (OR-bit)—to travel around an object in space; an orbit is also the path an object follows when circling an object in space.

scientist (SYE-un-tist)—a person who studies the world around us

telescope (TEL-uh-skohp)—a tool people use to look up at objects in space; telescopes make objects in space look closer than they really are.

tunnel (TUHN-uhl)—to create a narrow passageway through or under something